THIS BOOK BELONGS TO:

_____

WELCOME TO TEXAS

Dedicated to all the explorers.

All rights reserved.
No part of this book may be reproduced in any form or by any means, electronic or mechanical, and no photocopying or recording, unless you have written permission from the author.

ISBN 978-1-958985-35-9

Text copyright © 2024 by Mimi Jones

www.joeysavestheday.com

A Mimi Book

Texas got its name from the Caddo word "tejas," which means "friends" or "allies." Spanish missionaries had encountered the Caddo in the late 17th century and adopted the term which later evolved into "Texas."

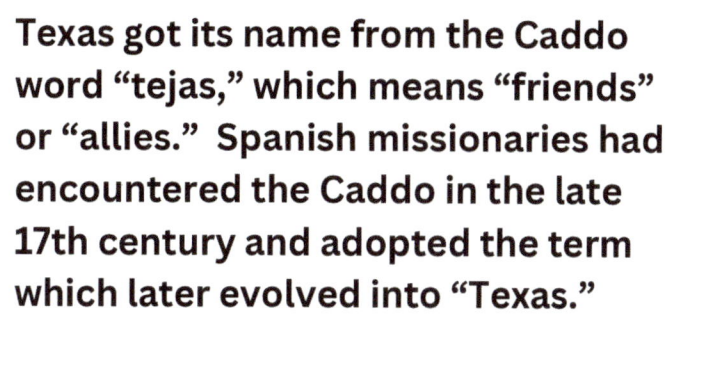

Texas was the twenty-eighth state to join the Union. It officially joined on December 29, 1845.

Texas is located in the South-Central region of the United States. Texas shares a border with four states: Arkansas, Louisiana, New Mexico, and Oklahoma. Texas also shares a border with Mexico.

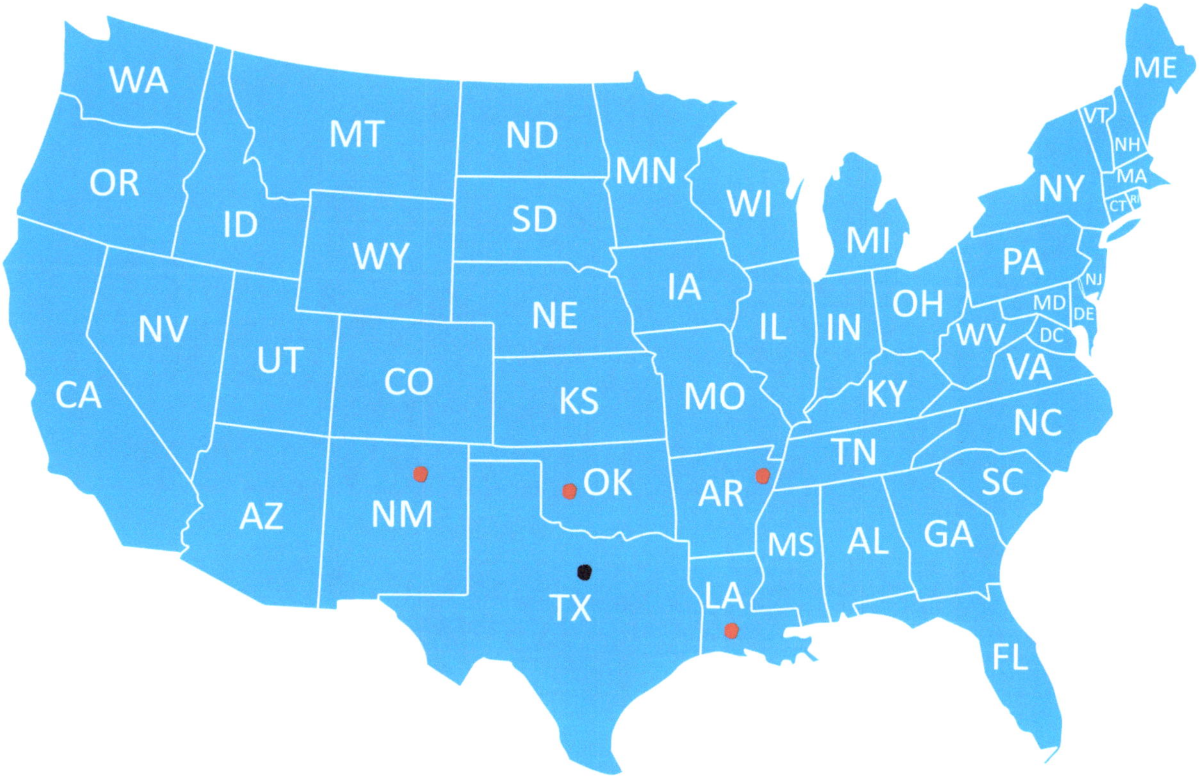

Austin is the capital of Texas.
It officially became the capital in 1839.

Austin, Texas, has an estimated population of about 964,175 people.

Texas is the second largest state in the United States. That means Texas comes in second place as one of the biggest states in the United States of America.

Texas State Capitol
1100 Congress Ave
Austin, TX 78701

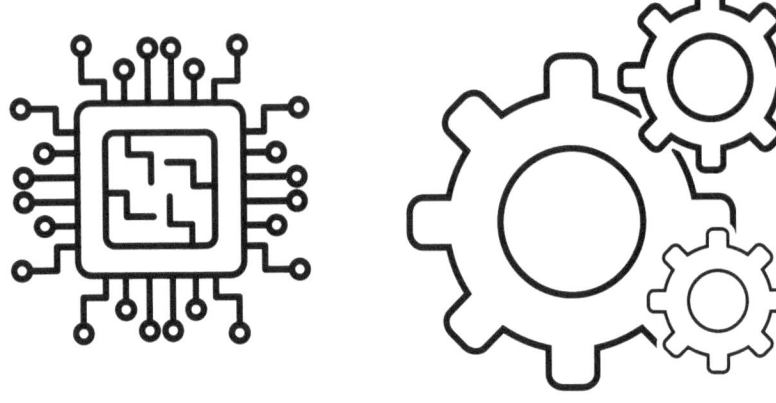

Jack Kilby was an electrical engineer who worked at Texas Instruments in Dallas, Texas. He invented the integrated circuit also known as a microchip and co-invented the thermal printer and handheld calculator.

Space Center Houston, located in Houston, Texas, is the official visitor center for NASA's Johnson Space Center. People can learn about space exploration and view over 400 space artifacts, including a Space Shuttle replica and a restored Saturn V rocket. Visitors can go on tours and touch a real moon rock.

Texas

There are 254 counties in Texas.

Here is a list of 20 of those counties:

Archer	Jefferson	Webb	Grayson
Fayette	Madison	Zavala	Eastland
Kent	Reagan	Montgomery	Cooke
Jones	Starr	Lynn	Andrews
El Paso	Washington	Hill	Coleman

Dr. Pepper, the popular soft drink was invented in 1885 in Waco, Texas by pharmacist Charles Alderton. He created it at Morrison's Old Corner Drug store by mixing different fruit and spice flavors.

South Padre Island is a popular tourist spot known for its beautiful beaches, clear waters, and vibrant atmosphere. Visitors can have fun playing water sports, fishing, watching dolphins, or eating local seafood.

Natural Bridge Caverns, near San Antonio, Texas, is one of the largest commercial caverns in the U.S. It was discovered in 1960 and features stunning underground formations. Visitors can go on guided tours, mine fossils and gems, and go zip-lining.

Big Bend National Park is located in southwest Texas along the Mexico border. The park features stunning desert, mountain, and river landscapes. It is home to many animals, including roadrunners and black bears. Visitors can hike, camp, stargaze, and birdwatch.

The Texas state bird is the Northern Mockingbird. It was chosen as the state bird in 1927.

The official state flower for Texas is the Bluebonnet. The Bluebonnet became the official state flower in 1901.

The Battle of Gonzales occurred in Gonzales, Texas, on October 2, 1835. This marked the initial confrontation in the Texas Revolution. The conflict arose over a cannon that the Mexicans sought to reclaim, but the Texians were determined to keep it.

A few nicknames for Texas are the Lone Star State, the Jumbo State, and the Beef State.

Lone Star State

JUMBO State

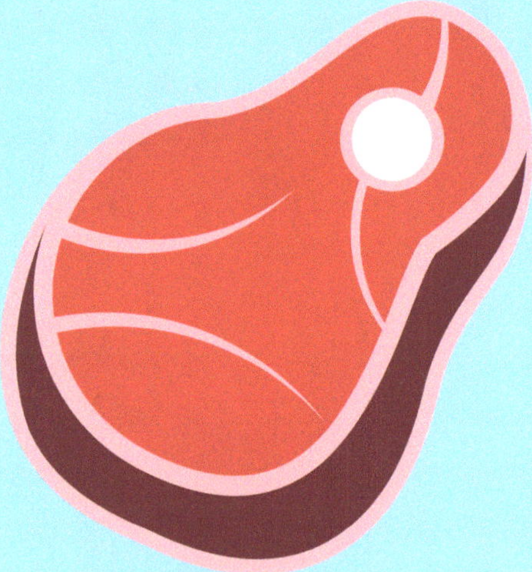

Beef State

The Texas state motto is "Friendship". The Texas state motto was adopted sometime in 1930.

The current state flag of Texas was officially adopted on January 25, 1839.

Some of the crops grown in Texas are beets, corn, cotton, cucumbers, peanuts, and rice.

Some of the animals that live in Texas include armadillos, bats, rattlesnakes, squirrels, and Texas Longhorns.

Texas experiences extreme temperatures. The highest recorded was 120 degrees Fahrenheit in Seymour, Texas, on August 12, 1936. The lowest was -23 degrees (23 degrees below zero) Fahrenheit in Tulia, Texas, on February 12, 1899.

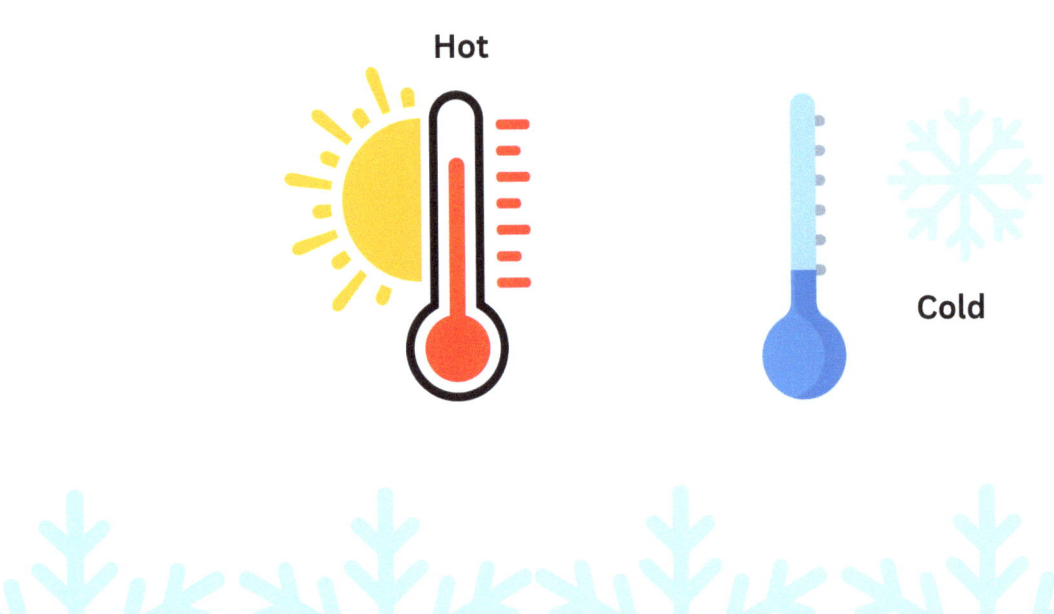

Hamilton Pool Preserve, near Dripping Springs, Texas, features a 50-foot waterfall that flows into a clear pool surrounded by greenery and limestone cliffs. Visitors can swim, hike, and picnic. However, reservations are required for entry.

Cadillac Ranch, near Amarillo, Texas, is a cool public art installation that was created in 1974. It features ten vintage Cadillac cars buried nose-first in the ground and covered with graffiti. It's a popular stop along Route 66.

Texas is home to the Texas Rangers, whose professional baseball team plays at Globe Life Field in Arlington.

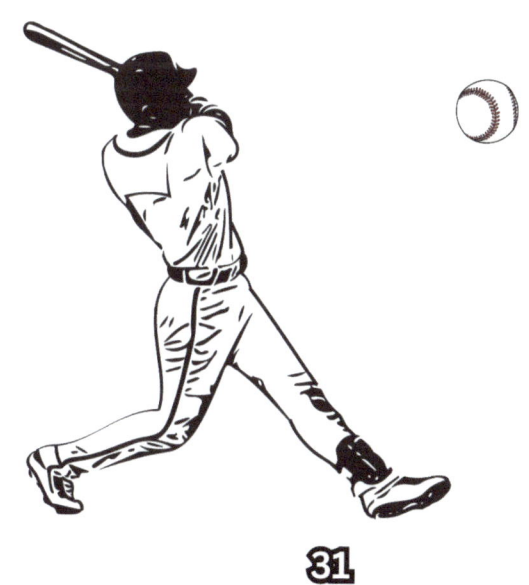

Texas is home to the University of Texas Longhorns, whose college football team plays at Darrell K Royal-Texas Memorial Stadium.

Dr. Denton A. Cooley, a renowned heart surgeon from Houston, Texas, performed the first successful U.S. heart transplant in 1968 and implanted the first total artificial heart in 1969.

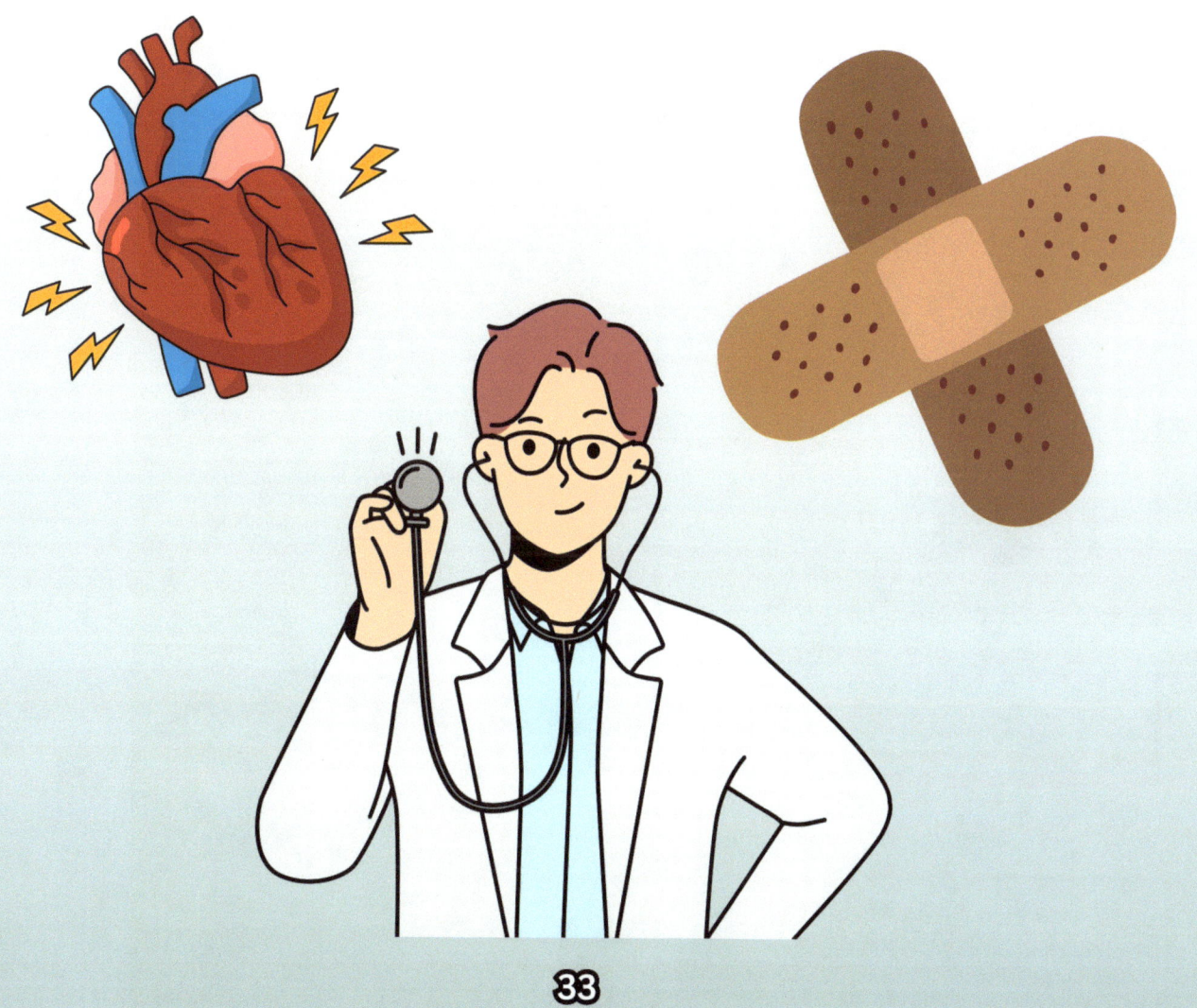

The Alamo in San Antonio, Texas, is famous for the 1836 battle during the Texas Revolution. Defenders like James Bowie and Davy Crockett fought General Santa Anna's larger Mexican army. Though defeated, the Alamo became a symbol of Texas independence. Today, it's a museum and landmark, drawing millions of visitors annually.

Can you name these?

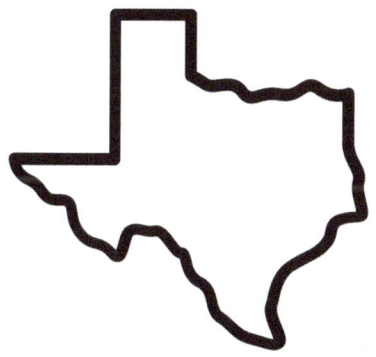

I hope you enjoyed learning about Texas.

To explore fun facts about the other 49 states, visit my website at www.joeysavestheday.com. You'll also find a wide variety of homeschool resources to support joyful learning at home. If you enjoyed this book, I would be grateful if you left a review. Your feedback truly helps. Thank you for your support!

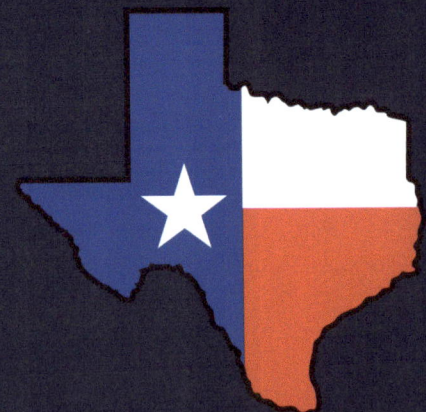

Check out these other interesting books in the 50 States Fact Books Series!

www.mimibooks.com